DIGITAL CAREER BUILDING™

CAREER BUILDING THROUGH

PODCASTING

SARAH SAWYER

ROSEN
PUBLISHING®

New York

*To Chris Osgood who taught—and teaches—me to think
creatively about networking and career building*

Published in 2008 by The Rosen Publishing Group, Inc.
29 East 21st Street, New York, NY 10010

First Edition

Library of Congress Cataloging-in-Publication Data

Sawyer, Sarah.
Career building through podcasting / Sarah Sawyer.
   p. cm. — (Digital career building)
Includes bibliographical references and index.
ISBN-13: 978-1-4042-1944-1 (library binding)
ISBN-10: 1-4042-1944-7 (library binding)
1. Podcasting—Vocational guidance—Juvenile literature.
2. Telecommunication—Vocational guidance—Juvenile literature.
3. Broadcasting—Vocational guidance—Juvenile literature. I. Title.
TK5102.6.S39 2008
070.5'7973--dc22

                        2007005442

Manufactured in the United States of America

CONTENTS

CHAPTER ONE

WHAT IS PODCASTING?

It seems that every computer user has a podcast these days—musicians, men who knit, and even the queen of England. That may leave you thinking, "If podcasts are so easily and frequently produced, how can there possibly be a career in podcasting? Isn't it just a hobby or a pastime, or another form of electronic communication, like e-mail, blogs, or MySpace?" The answers to these questions are simple. Not everyone knows how to podcast and not everyone who *does* know can do it well. It is possible to engage in podcasting for both fun and profit.

While the queen of England may podcast things like her annual Christmas speech, she does not build,

Queen Elizabeth II stands in London's Southward Cathedral after her 2006 Christmas broadcast, the first royal Christmas message ever podcasted.

upload, publicize, or distribute the podcast herself. A staff of public relations people and the sound and distribution professionals at the BBC (British Broadcasting System) do that for her. These people—the ones who make her podcasts happen—have careers in podcasting. If you play your cards right, so can you!

It's an exciting time to be starting off in a digital career. Congratulations for being wise enough to start exploring your career options so thoughtfully. You're already off to a great start! Now, on to the topic you are here to explore: career building through podcasting. But before you can build your career through podcasting, you'll need to know what podcasting is and why it's important.

What Is a Podcast?

Any broadcast created for play on a computer or a digital musical device (for example, an MP3 player such as the iPod) is a podcast. This includes radio-style shows created for distribution via the Internet, as well as television shows, movies, and radio broadcasts that are captured, stored, and redistributed online. Podcasts—or webcasts and netcasts, as they are sometimes called—can be instantly distributed to subscribers using RSS (Really Simple Syndication) feed. Subscribing via RSS makes the most recent edition of a podcast available to listeners whenever they decide to tune in.

Podcasting is a new form of communication, but it's not completely foreign. We have similar practices to compare it to. Your grandparents might relate podcasting to self-publishing a book. Your parents could

Information created for MP3 players can be accessed by almost anyone, anywhere, anytime. It is quickly becoming the easiest way to get material to an interested and specialized audience.

compare it to producing a community-access cable show. You might compare it to creating and distributing a zine. These are all ways in which individuals and groups of people create media that's intended to entertain or educate others on topics of shared interest. The one thing that ties them together is that they are independent forms of media. That is, these processes are used by those who work outside major media channels to broadcast or publish ideas without having to conform to editorial or business regulations. In essence, podcasters—like self-publishers, cable-access show creators, and zinesters—get their ideas out there without the help of established industry producers and

Loading "Podcasting News: The 2005 Word of the Year is....Podcast!"

http://www.podcastingnews.com/archives/2005/12/the_2005_word_o.html

Add Your Podcast : Feedback/Suggestions :

Podcasting NEWS

Podcasting News Home | Audio & Music News | Articles | Podcast Directory | Forum | Podcasting Gear | Podcasting Gear Manufacturers

« Odeo Gets Makeover | Main | Wikipedia Caught in Podfather Turf War »

The 2005 Word of the Year is....Podcast!

December 05, 2005

The Oxford University Press, publishers of the New Oxford American Dictionary, has selected **podcast** as the *Word of the Year* for 2005.

Erin McKean, editor in chief of the New Oxford American Dictionary, said: "Podcast was considered for inclusion last year, but we found that not enough people were using it, or were even familiar with the concept. This year it's a completely different story. The word has finally caught up with the rest of the iPod phenomenon."

"Choosing the word of the year is incredibly difficult," said McKean. "Not just because of the enormous amount of data we look at-everything from blogs to technical journals to suggestions sent to dictionaries@oup.com, but because everyone has such strong opinions about usage without being overly technical."

Oxford University Press defines podcast as "a digital recording of a radio broadcast or similar program, made available on the Internet for downloading to a personal audio player." While the Oxford definition would be considered incorrect by many podcasters, it reflects common usage without being overly technical.

"Podcast" will be added to the next online update of the New Oxford American Dictionary, due in early 2006.

Podcasting beat out several other words or phrases to be Word of the Year:

- bird flu (an often fatal flu virus of birds. esp. poultry, that is transmissible from them to humans, in whom it may also prove fatal)
- ICE (an entry stored in one's cellular phone that provides emergency contact information)
- IDP (internally displaced person; someone forced to relocate within a country because of a natural disaster or civil unrest)
- IED (improvised explosive device, such as a car bomb)
- lifehack (a more efficient or effective way of completing an everyday task: "I found a great lifehack for getting a cheap hotel room.")
- persistent vegetative state (a condition in which a patient recovering from a coma retains reflex responses and may appear wakeful, but has no cognitive functions or other evidence of cerebral cortical activity)
- reggaeton (a Latin American dance music which combines elements of reggae music with hip-hop and rap.)
- rootkit (software installed on a computer by someone other than the owner, intended to conceal other programs or processes, files or system data.)
- squick (cause immediate and thorough revulsion: "was anyone else squicked by our waiter's piercings?")
- sudoku (a logic-based puzzle consisting of squares that form grids within a grid. Into each smaller grid, the numerals 1 through 9 are entered but not repeated, and they may not be repeated in any row or column of the larger grid.)
- trans fat (fat containing trans-fatty acids, considered unhealthier than other dietary fats.)

Source: Oxford University Press

Podcastingnews.com, a web site devoted to podcasting-related news, a podcasting directory, and a user forum, reported on the word "podcast" being named "Word of the Year" by the New Oxford American Dictionary in 2005.

packagers. This means that you can use podcasts to say whatever you want. It is the ultimate in free speech and direct, unobstructed access to your audience.

Where Did the Podcast Get Its Name?

The word "podcast" was first used by Ben Hammersley in an article in the English newspaper the *Guardian* on February 12, 2004. He created the term by combining the words "iPod" and "broadcast." "Podcast" was quickly incorporated into the common language, and only a year later the *New Oxford American Dictionary* named it word of the year.

Some people wish a term other than "podcasting" had been used for the process. They worry that "podcasting" leads people to believe that you need an iPod to listen to podcasts. This is far from true. Any MP3 player—incorporated with or independent of a computer—will enable you to listen to podcasts. To make sure this point is understood, some people prefer to say "webcast" or "netcast" instead. Don't let that confuse you because these words have come to be used interchangeably; they all mean the same thing. Nevertheless, "podcast" still seems to be the most frequently used in relation to the process of uploading your personal audio and video content to shared sites.

The Cultural Context of Podcasting

Whenever people are arguing over a word, developing definitions for new processes or interests, or redefining terms, it is almost certainly a sign that a specific subculture is growing. If you're thinking of a career in podcasting, you probably already understand a lot about the cultural context of podcasting. Your knowledge of this context is a big part of what will make you so valuable to potential employers.

Your first step in understanding the cultural context of podcasting is understanding the meaning of the phrase "cultural context." It sounds complicated, but it's actually easy to understand. The word "culture" means a set of factors that shape a certain time and place to a certain group of people. For example, all the people and styles, facts and stories, fashions and recordings, songs and instruments in the world that relate to rock music,

Video podcasts, or vidcasts, of concerts and music videos, as well as audio podcasts of live and recorded music, have become some of the most popular kinds of podcasting content.

when grouped together, would be called rock culture. When you read about a favorite rock star or learn a new song, you are learning about a tiny piece of rock culture. If you start a band, write a song, or become a big fan of a band or song, then you actually become a part of rock culture yourself. You are learning about, participating in, and keeping alive an interest in and use of a certain type of thing: rock music. By doing so, you're furthering and enriching rock culture.

Just like rock fans, Internet users have developed—and continue to develop—a culture of their own. Internet culture is popular and ever-growing. If you use the Internet, you are already a part of it. You probably know

Electronic media is the major way in which people tap into global pop culture. Devices like MP3 players and BlackBerrys put you in contact with the world, even if you haven't left school grounds

a lot about Internet culture already, without necessarily being aware that you were being initiated into it. You just thought you were picking up something new in a natural and easy way.

Do you know what TTYL means? Do you know what a blog is? Do you know what an IM is? Do you IM? If the answer to any or all of these questions is yes, then congratulations! You know all about and are a part of Internet culture. That involvement is the first thing you need in order to build a career in podcasting.

Basic computer and Internet literacy might be common to you and your friends, but it's not common to everyone in the workforce. Think about the other people in your family and what they know—or don't know— about the Internet and the way things are done online. Is what you know about the Internet the same as what your parents and grandparents know? Probably not. That can be exciting because it puts you at an advantage in the job market. Your knowledge of Internet culture is a valuable skill.

Your parents probably remember the first time they used a computer and got on the Internet. They may have used an early-model Apple computer. Computers were very different back then. They were not as user-friendly and most likely did not have an Internet connection.

Not too long ago, there were a lot fewer Web sites. The ones that did exist were mostly owned by schools, businesses, and government organizations. Most people used the Internet only for e-mail and business commu-nications. They didn't converse, shop, or surf the way they do today, and they certainly didn't contribute their own content via message boards, blogs, personal Web sites, or podcasts. That phenomenon occurred within only the last decade or so. This cultural devel-opment is referred to as Web 2.0 because it is the second big development in Internet culture (following the creation of the Internet itself), and you are a part of it!

Web 2.0 and Podcasting

Podcasts are a new way of helping people do some-thing they've done for millennia: communicate. Before podcasts, there were print periodicals like newspapers and magazines, broadcast radio and television shows, and even things like HAM radios that allowed people to take to the airwaves. People could record their voices onto tape and CD. But it was not until the podcast that they could create a recording that was not subject to FCC (Federal Communications Commission) regulations, editorial processes, and distribution challenges. This was the first time ordinary people could record themselves communicating freely and make it available—often at no charge—to anyone on Earth with an MP3 player and a desire to listen. It was also the first time that people have been able to have programming delivered to them automatically via RSS and stored for them to listen to whenever they want.

It's easy not to be immediately impressed by the advent of podcasting because many of us have become so accustomed to the regular arrival of new technology over the last two decades. But this development is worth getting excited about. Why? Because it opens up career possibilities—and advantages—to you!

Before podcasts, if you had a very specialized interest and wanted to share it with people, you had to convince a newspaper to publish your article on it; persuade a radio host to interview you; win an interview on television or cable access; or find some other way to get someone else to connect you to your audience. More recently, people started to publish and distribute zines—low-budget, self-produced magazines. They also connected with other zine enthusiasts who would help them with their product. Writing, designing, publishing, and producing zines is a big undertaking

Creating an audio show used to require a sound studio. Today, podcasting makes it possible for anyone with a computer and an Internet connection to share his or her ideas and entertain an interested audience.

that requires enormous effort. Today, podcasts offer a simpler, easier way to get your content out there. It's almost as simple as pressing a few buttons on your keyboard.

CHAPTER TWO

A HOW-TO GUIDE TO PODCASTING

Think of all the ways you can use a podcast. Want to teach people about your interests? Eager to get your band's demo into the right hands? Want to let people know about exciting things they can do if they take your class, buy your product, or join your club? Looking to entertain? All you have to do is record and post your podcast. It's that simple. It's revolutionary and it allows you to build an exciting career for yourself.

How to Produce a Podcast

The basics of producing a podcast are reduced to a relatively simple set of steps.

What is required today for a podcast pales in comparison to the amount of equipment needed to make studio-quality recordings even ten years ago.

15

1. Plan your podcast: Choose content and write an outline or script to work from.
2. Record, edit, and save your podcast in MP3 format: There are any number of software options you can use to simplify this process. Some popular choices are Garageband, Wavepad, and Audacity.
3. Upload the audio MP3 file and summarize the show, add meta tagging, and create the RSS feed file.
4. Publish and host your podcast and RSS feed using your own site or a podcasting publishing and hosting service.

You've just created a podcast! Podcasting software and services make this process easy. As software and Web resources are developed, this process will change and become even easier. The hard part is choosing and offering quality content.

Choosing Content

Content is subject matter. It's anything you say, quote, or show to an audience. People tune in to your podcast so that they can hear (or see) your content, so it's important that you choose it well. If your content or message is not interesting or well chosen, your audience will lose interest and discontinue their subscriptions to your podcast.

Byte-Sized Topics

Your series of podcasts should have a central topic. For the purpose of this discussion, let's pretend that topic is ballroom dancing. In a broad sense, all your podcasts will be

Podcasting is an easy way to discover new bands and share your favorite music with others.

about ballroom dancing, but each episode will need to be about some smaller topic within that topic. Such topics might include descriptions of dance steps, reviews of local dance clubs, music suggestions, buying dance shoes, preparing for competitions, finding a great teacher, etc.

Before you launch a podcast, it might be a good idea to make a list of possible episode topics. This will give you an idea of whether or not your topic is broad enough to support the number of episodes you plan to produce. Try this with different topics just for practice. After a few tries you'll have a better idea of which topics are broad enough to support an ongoing podcast and which ones are too specialized.

Just because you have enough ideas for a series of podcasts doesn't mean the content you've chosen will attract a large audience. To get a better idea of what attracts and keeps an audience, spend some time thinking about what interests you. Chances are, if you are intrigued about a certain topic or activity, a number of other people are as well. They will want to learn more or feel connected to fellow enthusiasts.

Listen for Form and Function

Pay attention to the podcasts that you enjoy. Take time to notice what sort of content they offer and in what manner they present it. Do you notice that podcasts of one length feel too long and ones of another length seem too short? Do you find yourself bored by one style of presentation and really entertained by a different style? You will be able to gather lots of information about the kind of podcast you want to create from the types of podcasts you like listening to. You can base your podcast on the form of another podcast. For example, if your favorite podcast is a piece of capsule information or a discussion sandwiched between a theme song and an invitation to subscribe, your podcast might use the same formula, enhanced by your own thoughts, words, perspective, and subject matter.

Popular podcasts, ones that you like, and those that are rated highly by groups you trust are great resources when it comes to building a successful podcast. They can serve as useful models for podcasts you will create in the future. They can help keep you on track.

Social networking sites like MySpace.com are a great way to connect with others who might want to listen to your podcast. Use the same safety rules in podcasting that you have learned to use for social sites.

Think Before You Speak

Consider your content carefully before you post it on the Web. Once published, your podcast has a life of its own, one that is now beyond your control. Make sure the content is free of material that could be damaging to you now or in the future. As always when connected to the Internet, do not give away any personal information and think carefully before sharing controversial or dangerous views. There may come a time in your social, religious, or professional life when you wish there was not a record of the things a "younger you" said and did. Many podcasts are intended for a small and specialized audience—such as your circle of friends—but it is always possible that you will touch on a hot topic that catches the interest of a much larger audience.

If you're confused as to what content is appropriate and safe to post, consult with your parents or another trusted adult. Hopefully they can help you think through possibilities and choose the best course of action.

Script Your Show

After you've settled on some content but before you turn on the microphone and begin recording, take the time to script your episode. Some people write down every word they want to say; others write down key points and then improvise, or "wing it." Either is fine as long as it helps you map out your podcast in advance and stay on track while you're actually recording. Try both methods—or a mix of methods—and see what works best for you.

Practice, Practice, Practice!

Once you've scripted your show, rehearse it a few times. See if you like how it sounds and feels as you rehearse. This is a great time to make changes if you want to. It's also a great opportunity to determine if your podcast will fit within the timeframe you've planned, without running long or short. If you find that it is too long or too short, this is the perfect time to make adjustments.

"Lay It in Wax"

In the days when people recorded sound onto records, or LPs ("long-players"), they actually used wax and referred

Internet Safety

The National Center for Missing and Exploited Children is dedicated to keeping young people safe from predators. Its Web site offers these guidelines for keeping safe while blogging or using social networking sites. While they don't mention podcasting specifically, the same guidelines will help you podcast safely.

- Never post your personal information, such as cell phone number, address, or the name of your school.
- Be aware that information you give out could also put you at risk for victimization. People looking to harm you could use the information you post to gain your trust. They can also deceive you by pretending they know you.
- Never give out your password to anyone other than your parent or guardian.
- Only add people as friends to your site if you know them in real life.
- Never meet in person with anyone you first "met" on a social networking site. Some people may not be who they say they are.
- Think before posting your photos. Personal photos should not have revealing information, such as school names or locations. Look at the backgrounds of the pictures to make sure you are not giving out any identifying information without realizing it. The name of a mall, the license plate of your car, street signs, or the name of your sports team on your clothing all contain information that can give your location away.
- Never respond to harassing or rude comments posted to your site.
- Remember that posting information about your friends could put them at risk. Protect your friends by not posting any names, ages, phone numbers, school names, or locations. Refrain from making or posting plans and activities on your site.

Today's technology makes recording and distributing files as easy as pressing a button or plugging in an adaptor.

to the recording process as "laying it in wax." Today, of course, we're using computers to record sound and are "laying it" in silicone. The process you'll go through to record your podcast will vary depending on the software you use. The best way to learn how to make the most of your software is to take the tutorial offered by the software company. It will walk you though the features of the system and the technical process. It may feel like a big-time commitment, especially if you're used to just diving in to new applications, but knowing how to use your tools correctly is well worth it in the long run. It may save you the trouble of losing your recording or having to re-record.

Visit the resources section in the back of this book for a listing of podcasting software and online tutorial resources. These resources will explain the nuts and bolts of creating a podcast.

CHAPTER THREE

PODCASTING AS A CAREER

It's hard to say exactly what sort of future careers might include podcasting because Web 2.0 is still fairly new, and podcasting is still developing at an amazing rate. What this means to young people planning for careers in the field is that over the next few years, the culture will grow and change. Some possibilities that are open now will not exist in a few years, and positions that do not exist now will open up throughout the industry. The best way to start career building is to keep current on podcasting culture and the people who make it happen.

Today, most podcasters are hobbyists who create podcasts on topics that interest them simply for the joy of doing it. In these cases, money generally doesn't enter

Andrew Sims, 17, hosts his award-winning podcast, MuggleCast, from his bedroom in Medford, New Jersey.

the picture. They do it for personal enjoyment, but occasionally someone creates a podcast that gets a lot of attention and begins to turn a profit. These people are the superstars of podcasting.

Superstars of Podcasting

A few podcasters create a significant and lasting online sensation. This attention and popularity then attracts advertisers. Related businesses will sometimes pay a podcaster to mention their products and services, or they may buy space on the podcaster's Web site. It could be that a very popular podcast would charge listeners to subscribe. In these cases, the podcast would generate some income. The amount of income would vary greatly depending on a variety of factors.

Teen podcasters Andrew Sims and Ben Shoen are prime examples of this profitable scenario. These dedicated fans of the teen literary character Harry Potter podcast a weekly show in which they broadcast news regarding J. K. Rowling's series of novels and discuss things they think will happen next. Their podcast—called MuggleCast—is so popular that GoDaddy.com offered them a partnership in which they make $15 for every new member their podcast brings to GoDaddy. This is not a huge income, but it will earn them some spending money and it is a very impressive marketing project that's sure to attract the attention of college admissions officers and future employers.

For a real podcast-related profit explosion, look no further than BoingBoing.net and its video documenting what happens when Diet Coke and Mentos candies are

 Companies like GoDaddy.com make great hosts for podcasters. They have even partnered with podcasters like Andrew Sims to make the medium profitable for host and podcaster alike.

mixed together. In 2006, BoingBoing.net named Fritz Grove and Stephen Voltz "Top Earners" in its New Media Power List for the Diet Coke and Mentos experiments the two podcasted via EepyBird.com. Their podcast was viewed more than five million times, was featured on national broadcast news and entertainment channels, and was picked up by a wide sampling of Internet news sites and link pages. These savvy performers/scientists made almost $30,000 from a Web site that hosted their filmed experiments.

A CLOSER LOOK There's more to judging the long-term profitability of a career than taking one very successful podcast's net profit into

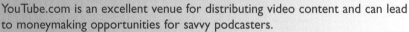

YouTube.com is an excellent venue for distributing video content and can lead to moneymaking opportunities for savvy podcasters.

consideration. In order to keep that kind of money coming in on a regular basis, you would have to create profitable hit after profitable hit. While that certainly is possible, the odds are simply against you. The Diet Coke and Mentos podcast is one out of millions of podcasts created and posted daily by people all over the world. For every podcast that turns a profit, you must remember that the vast majority never make a penny.

This is not meant to discourage you. It's just food for thought. There is a profit to be made by podcasting, but it isn't always steady and come in the form of cash. The real payoff from podcasting may be the career possibilities that open up for you once you've developed some podcasting skills.

Free Your Mind and Your Podcast Will Follow

Being an Internet superstar isn't the only way you can make money podcasting. You might work behind the scenes by helping another person or a company produce a podcast. Jobs like these tend to be a good fit for people who are more excited about the medium of podcasting than about the content topic they'd be podcasting. To find out if you're one of those people, ask yourself this: Would podcasting be as much fun if it were on a topic that held very little interest for you? If you answer no, then maybe you are someone who is driven by the subject matter and not by the medium of podcasting. If, however, you find yourself answering, "Well, yes. Maybe I would be as interested in the process and technology of podcasting as in the content," then it's possible that you have what it takes to help others produce and distribute podcasts.

Let's say a business near you wants to podcast but doesn't know how. In that case, they might hire people like you to take care of everything technically related to the podcast (while they handle the content creation). You would help them organize and plan material. You would help them to produce the highest-quality sound possible. You would post the podcast, publicize it, oversee subscriptions, and probably help out in a whole host of other ways. You'd serve in much the same capacity as a radio or television producer, and you'd need to know all aspects of podcasting.

Maybe you aren't interested in the technical or logistical aspects of podcasting, but you really shine

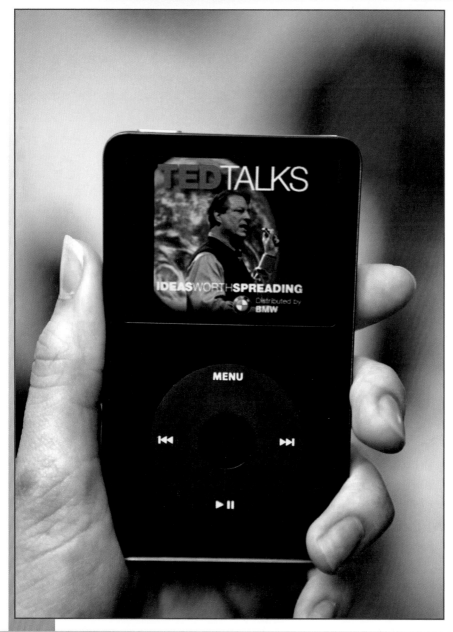

Video podcasts, or vidcasts, are as easy to access on video-ready MP3 players as are audio podcasts, and they're completely portable. You can have a high-quality viewing experience anywhere you go.

when it comes to performing. People compliment your voice all of the time and say that you're quite funny, thought-provoking, or unique. If there's someone who really wants to podcast but is shy and can't bear the thought of being recorded, videotaped, or photographed, that person might hire you to do voice-over work or perform a podcast for him or her.

Perhaps what really excites you is the quickly evolving networking culture of podcasting. You love to listen to different kinds of podcasts, and you're interested in what makes them successes or failures. You have a knack for knowing what the next hot things will be, and you have an easy time identifying and explaining what those are and why they are about to emerge as popular trends. If that sounds like you, you might enjoy working as a consultant, market analyst, and trendspotter for people and businesses who want to podcast.

In this capacity, you would meet with those who want to podcast but haven't yet learned how to create one themselves. You would talk them through what they need to know to create a podcast that will achieve the goals they have for it. They may hope for a certain number of subscribers or a certain level of Internet attention. You will help them make a realistic, workable plan that will help them reach their goals, and you will determine if they are meeting their goals or not.

Your clients will rely on you to identify and be knowledgeable about all the hottest podcasting and Internet technology developments and trends. They will count on you to know the best way to get their message across to listeners. They may hire you directly or through an electronic media firm that specializes in creating Web pages, e-mail newsletters, podcasts, and other forms of online communication.

Can't decide between all the possibilities before you? That's OK! During the course of your career, you will likely find yourself working on different projects in different capacities. Each project will teach you something new or sharpen another set of skills. Each will lead you to fresh and hopefully better projects. It's all a matter of keeping both your mind and your eyes open to possibilities.

Build Your Professional Network Through Podcasting

There's lots of talk about networking in almost every business setting. It sounds complicated, but it's really just a new way of talking about an old idea. Have you ever heard someone say, "It's not what you know, it's who you know"? There's no doubt about it—knowing people in the right places can help you get things done much more quickly. Think for a moment about how things work at your school or in your community center. You wouldn't ask your drama coach about yesterday's math assignment, would you? Probably not. Your math teacher is the one who made the assignment, so your math teacher is the person to ask about it. Networking operates in the same way. It's just the art of knowing people, and letting them know you, so that you can make things happen. Podcasting can help you do that.

Podcasting conferences and other digital technology trade shows can open up great networking opportunities for young professionals and can create the chance for you to connect with people you want to work with most.

For instance, if you have a passion for salsa dancing and want to build a career teaching dance lessons, you might produce a podcast on salsa dancing. You might mention in your podcast that you are accepting students. People who hear your podcast will discover that you know something about salsa dancing and are offering lessons. If your listeners are in your area and want to take lessons, they know whom to call.

When you podcast a show on a certain topic, you can present yourself as an authority because you are sharing your expertise on the subject with others. Interested people will listen to your podcast and learn something about you and your expertise. Then, if one of these listeners is in a position to hire someone with your knowledge, he or she won't need to look beyond their MP3 player to find the right person: YOU!

Perhaps a magazine editor will hear your podcast on a book you've read, a profile of a favorite author, or a movie review. If impressed, he or she may contact you and ask you to write an article for his or her publication. Perhaps a youth group leader will hear your podcast and invite you to make a presentation to his group. Maybe your favorite high-profile podcaster will hear your podcast and invite you to be a guest on his or her show.

Now take a moment to see if there's any way you can help a situation like that along. Is there someone you admire and would like to meet? Do you think it would be appropriate to send the person an e-mail and invite him or her to listen to your podcast? If you're not sure, ask a trusted adult for his or her opinion.

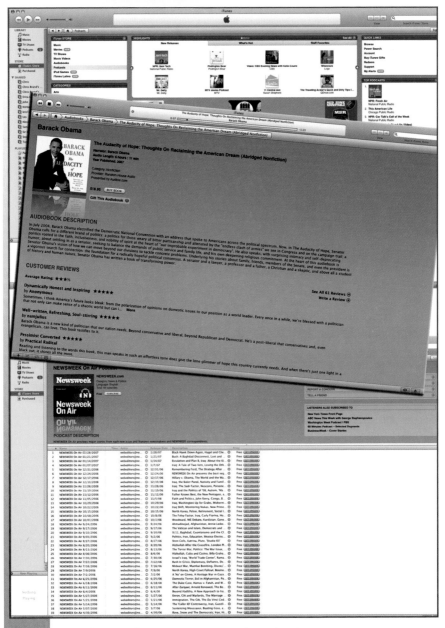

Apple's iTunes makes keeping track of podcasts, music, videos, and even audiobooks easier. Enter a name—in this case, 2008 presidential candidate Barack Obama—and iTunes will point you to lots of available content.

What you're learning right now is networking. It's how people—especially those who earn a living in the field of electronic media—connect with each other and make things happen.

CHAPTER FOUR

BUILDING A
PODCASTING CAREER

Has reading this book inspired you to daydream about pursuing a career in podcasting? That's excellent! Many great men and women have gotten their best and most creative ideas by daydreaming. Know that your dreams are about to look more like reality because no matter what kind of career you're imagining, there are many things you do today that will get you closer to achieving your dreams in the future.

Best Practices

If you're reading this book, you probably see a way podcasting can fit into the career of your choice. In order to make the actions you take today as effective as possible,

PodBlaze.com, and services like it, are great hosting, networking, and advertising resources for podcasters.

FreshPodcasts.com is a great way to host podcasts or find new ones to listen to. It makes getting familiar with best practices easy and fun.

you'll need to do one thing: become the best podcaster you can be. But what makes a good podcaster? The answer to this question is somewhat subjective. Yet as varied as people's tastes can be, there are a few points upon which everyone in the know can agree. These points are often referred to as "best practices," and they're a great place to start your journey toward becoming the best podcaster possible.

Best practices are generally widely recognized qualities that make something work as well as it possibly can. Rodney L. Rumford, the founder of PodBlaze.com and FreshPodcasts.com, lists the following best practices in his white paper "What You Don't Know About Podcasting

Could Hurt Your Business: How to Leverage and Benefit from This New Media Technology." Rumford knows plenty about the field of podcasting and what the people who hire him to work on their podcasts perceive to be important.

As you read this list, think about which of these best practices you know how to do and which you might need to develop or improve upon. When you come across a skill you'd like to develop, take a moment to brainstorm places you might acquire it (i.e., college classes, apprenticeships with a professional, workshops, community education classes, Web site tutorials, trade or technical publications, print or Web articles, etc.). Take notes as you read. These notes are about to become your personalized to-do list for becoming a fantastic podcasting professional.

Podcasting Best Practices from Rodney L. Rumford

1. Know your audience/target market.
2. Be organized in the messaging that is to be delivered.
3. Have notes and an outline to keep the show on topic.
4. Edit show appropriately for content, quality, and length.
5. Deliver valuable, informative, engaging, and entertaining content to your listeners that they can't get from any other media.
6. Ensure good-quality audio by using proper recording hardware and software.
7. Provide show notes for listeners to review content of the show before and while they listen to the podcast.
8. Use proper tagging of meta data so that your podcast can be found and organized easily by podcasting software and directories.

9. Ensure that the RSS feed for the podcast is valid and in compliance with the 2.0 standard. Additional functionality is required if you want the podcast to be iTunes-compatible.
10. Submit your podcast to the popular directories so that it can reach a greater audience.
11. Ping (notify) the major podcasting, RSS, and blog directories after each podcast to ensure that your podcasts are updated.
12. Have the proper Web server technology that can deliver the content quickly and handle the server bandwidth issues.
13. Have an experienced podcasting consultant design, map, and oversee the entire process to ensure success the first time.

The More You Learn, the More You Learn How Much You Still Have to Learn

It never fails: When you start to learn about something you love, you learn that there is much more to know about it than you'd first thought. Remember when you began playing your favorite sport? You were probably only interested in learning how to hit the ball or make a basket. Now that you've been a fan of that sport for some time, you're probably aware of how many rules, techniques, statistics, and bits of trivia there are to know. You could learn about your interest—whether it is sports, art, literature, music, video games, comics, or computer technology—over the course of an entire lifetime. That's what makes it fun and ever-interesting. Podcasting is the same way. No matter how much you know, there will always be more to learn. Don't be afraid to keep learning. That's what separates the professionals from the amateurs.

First, take a moment to consider how your podcasting process measures up to the process detailed in the above list. Are there things on this list that you already do? Are there things on this list that you could use a little help improving upon? Are there items on this list you think could take you years to learn how to do well? Make notes next to the best practices that you don't know how to do yet. Take a moment to consider where you might learn to do them. Perhaps there's a free online tutorial that could teach you what you need to know. Maybe there's a library book that would help. Would a broadcasting class expand and build upon your knowledge base? Would an internship at a local radio station help you acquire the sound skills you'd like to have? Could an acting or improvisation coach help you develop your vocal and presentation skills? Could an informational interview with a more experienced electronic media professional help you plot where you might want to take your career. Write down all the possibilities you can think of. Carry this list with you—new ideas will come to you over time.

This exercise is a great way to remind yourself what skills future employers are looking for in a podcasting professional and to help you gauge how far you still have to go to acquiring those skills. It also helps you to discover ways to get the qualifications you need. Is there something on the list that jumps out at you because it looks like it would be fun, useful, or easy to accomplish?

Internet searches from home can lead you to great sources of information, but they can never replace your local library. Librarians provide great expertise on your subject of interest, whether it be in books or the Internet.

If so, you may have found your next step toward becoming the kind of podcasting professional you want to be.

Helpful Hints

Add the following tips to your surfing to do list over the next few years. They will help you stay current on best practices and professional opportunities.

Keep an eye out for new best practices: Internet culture develops quickly. It's a good idea to search for best practices periodically and see if they've changed, and if your to-do list needs to change accordingly.

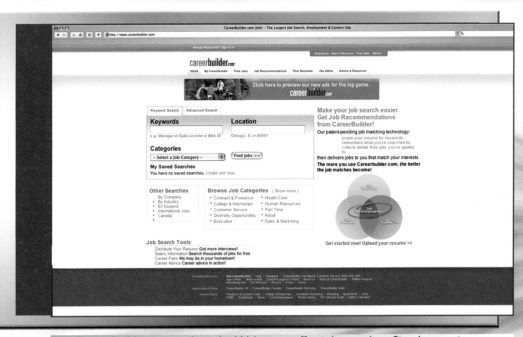

CareerBuilder.com and similar Web sites offer job searches. Simply type in keywords that interest you, and they'll e-mail you current openings. It's a great way to learn more about the job market for digital professionals.

Read the want ads: Employment-oriented Web sites like Monster, CareerBuilder, HotJobs, and the online "Help Wanted" sections of most newspapers allow you to run a search of current job listings based on key words. They also will e-mail you new listings that fit your search requirements. Enter "podcast" or "podcasting" as a key word and see what comes up. Even though you may not be ready to take a full-time job or even start interviewing, it's a good idea to read these ads. From them, you'll get a better idea of what employers are looking for in job candidates. You will realize what sort of skills you will need to be competitive in the market. You may also get the contact information of

Craigslist.com lists available full-time jobs and "gigs," which are limited-term, project-based jobs. These gigs offer young people the opportunity to gain valuable work experience that doesn't interfere with school.

someone you'd like to meet with for an informational interview.

Watch for "gigs": On message boards like Craigslist. com, the "gigs" section is used for one-time-only, freelance jobs. Watch that section for people who need podcasting help. You may find a limited-term job that fits your knowledge base and your schedule. Keep track of these gigs. You can add them to your résumé when you're ready to look for full-time, permanent work. Keep copies of the podcasts you have helped create and of the contact information of your clients. If the gig goes well, you can show the work to potential clients, and your old clients may be willing to act as references for you.

Professionalism

The word "professional" can mean lots of things. Actors and athletes consider themselves professional the first time they get paid to perform. Doctors, lawyers, and others in careers that require extensive training are referred to as professionals once they've completed years of school work or a certification program, or both.

In some ways, calling yourself professional means you are working and being paid for your work. It can imply more than that, though. When you say you are professional, or you talk about professionalism, people will expect a certain type of behavior from you. They will expect you to be polite, on time, and able to meet your deadlines. They will expect you to finish what you start and do what you say you're going to do. They will expect you to be consistent and good at what you do. All of these things together make up a "work ethic"—the way you feel about work and how you conduct yourself when you're working.

This is a great time to start conducting yourself like a professional. To learn more about what that means, seek out the working professionals around you. If there's someone who does the kind of work you'd like to do, e-mail or call the person and ask about the nature of the work, his or her duties and responsibilities, and the ways in which the person is expected to conduct him- or herself. Ask your teachers, parents,

An important aspect of professionalism is the ability to work well with other people, successfully complete group projects, and listen to and respect each other's opinions and ideas.

and friends with jobs. Take time to notice how their answers differ and how they are the same. Judge the value of their insights based on their own career achievements and their success in the workplace.

CHAPTER FIVE

PODCASTING YOUR WAY TO SUCCESS

You may choose to podcast professionally. You may also use your podcasting skills to explore another media-related profession. Web 2.0 makes it possible to do that through viral marketing.

"Viral marketing" is the term people use to refer to the phenomenon of letting others know about you or your product by creating a piece of new media that is exciting enough to inspire them to e-mail or otherwise share links to it with their friends. If your podcast begins to be shared by a growing number of computer users, it can really catch fire, "go viral," and end up being viewed by thousands or even millions of people, including influential media executives.

OK Go's wildly popular "treadmill" video for their song "Here It Goes Again" is part of a low-budget movement that's changing how music is marketed.

The Chicago-based band OK Go made brilliant use of viral marketing. They created a fun video of themselves dancing on treadmills, and it made people think, "Who are these guys?" They were one of the first music groups to use podcasting and viral marketing to further their careers.

OK Go made succeeding at viral marketing look easy. Damian Kulash, the band's lead singer, was quoted in a recent *USA Today* article saying, "I could not have dreamed of a weirder world, where the highest of top brass at our label and parent company are going, like, 'Can you guys do something really low-fi in your backyard again?'"

Kulash isn't the only one who recognizes and marvels at the "weirder world" we're living in. Kevin Maney, a technology columnist for *USA Today*, recognized the growing phenomenon, too. He wrote to the business people involved to ask about the effects of OK Go's viral marketing success. The band's manager, Jamie Lincoln Kitman, answered him in an e-mail, writing, "This is a paradigm smasher of the first order. . . The labels will have to get this sort of democracy-in-action under their thumb soon, but for now. . . wow." That's good news for you. That means the media people who are making things happen are listening to the power of the podcast, and you have a good chance of getting their attention.

More evidence of the success of this viral podcast phenomenon came to Maney in the form of an e-mail from EMI spokesman Adam Grossberg. In it, Grossberg lists numbers that point to OK Go's success

Damian Kulash, Tim Nordwind, Dan Konopka, and Andy Ross of the band OK Go are pioneers in the world of viral marketing via podcasts, thanks to their video for "Here It Goes Again," which became an Internet phenomenon.

(as quoted in Maney's article "OK Go: Masters of the YouTube Age"):

- Since putting up the video on YouTube four weeks ago, the video has been viewed more than 3.5 million times.
- "Here It Goes Again" is by far the biggest video of the month, and it has already cracked into YouTube's top 10 videos of all time.
- As a result of this response, the album went into the iTunes Top 30 (it's still hovering there).
- OK Go saw a 182 percent jump on Billboard's Digital Album chart during the week of August 13—advancing to #30 on the chart from nowhere.
- The very same week the band rocketed from #124 to #29 on Billboard's Heatseeker chart, thanks to a 102 percent increase in scans. Capitol's sales department has another 50,000 units shipping out to stores.
- And the band was just confirmed to do the very same routine—live on stage at MTV's Video Music Awards.

What we learn from OK Go's example is that it is possible to boost your success in a non-digital field (such as popular music) by making the most of podcasting and other forms of viral communication. The same principles would work for someone trying to build an audience as a stunt person, comic, poet, or politician. A writer could create a piece that gets passed around and gets editors and publishers interested in the manuscript he or she has written. An athlete could create an eye-catching podcast that might make it into the hands of a coach or scout looking for his or her team's next superstar. The possibilities are endless.

It sounds easy, right? But if it were really that easy, everyone would be doing it and we'd all be rock stars. The truth is that OK Go's plan worked for OK Go. While they've blazed a trail and indicated a viable path that others can try to follow, it will probably be a long time before lightning strikes again and someone else recording a low-budget video makes it huge. The next successful viral marketer will need to come up with his or her own creative, trendsetting idea. But the process will be somewhat the same. They will create something fun, fresh, and exciting; lots of people will pass it around; and, eventually, big media companies will want a part of it and be willing to pay for it.

Your best chance at success with this type of marketing will come from adapting what has worked for other people to your product, while bringing your sense of creativity and innovation to the process. No one can tell you exactly how to create a podcast that will "go viral"—you'll have to follow your instincts and try for yourself. There are things you can do, however, to make your trial and error more effective.

Make Something You Like

If you like it, chances are good someone else will like it, too.

Keep Records and Watch Trends

If you produce and release podcasts and don't pay attention to the user results, you'll be missing out on a very useful block of information. The software you're using will likely offer ways to manage your subscriber list

Habits you form today can serve you well throughout your professional life. Reading trade publications, like *Wired* magazine (WiredMagazine.com), can help you stay current on professional trends, best practices, and new technology.

and track the number of downloads. Watch these numbers to see if they go up or down, and then check to see if there's anything you do that affects them. For example, if your numbers are higher when you're posting often but drop off when you post less frequently, then you've learned that your audience likes it when your podcast is kept up to date.

If people forward the podcasts you've scripted but don't tend to forward the ones in which you improvise, then you've learned that your scripted podcasts yield the best results. When you clearly determine what gets the best results with your audience, then you have a better chance of producing successful work in the future.

Document and Save Your Body of Work

When viewed together, your podcasts are called your body of work. Always back up your podcasts onto a disk and keep them in a safe place. Then you'll have a complete archive of your body of work to use whenever you need it.

You'll use your body of work in lots of ways, so it's good to keep it safe and carefully and accurately labeled and annotated. Keep notes with your documented copies that describe the subject matter, creation date, original podcast date, time, and anything you notice about how the podcasts were received and responded to. If it's a podcast you do for others, make notes about what they asked for, how you helped them, and the success (or failure) of the podcast. Make notes next to the podcasts that you are most proud of or that you think achieved the best results. Take the time to write yourself a note about

Document your work and back it up on a CD. You never know when you'll want to show a particular piece to a potential employer. This habit will ensure that you have your entire body of work at your fingertips if and when you need it.

why you think that podcast is a great example of your overall work and abilities. This will help you decide which podcasts to include when you're putting together a portfolio and résumé. You'll know which podcasts to show in order to give potential clients the best possible idea of what you do.

This practice will also be helpful to you as a podcaster. When you review your entire body of work, you can chart your own growth. You can compare the work you used to do with the work you do now and see how you've developed. You will also begin to identify your strongest skills and the ones you still need to work harder on.

Never Stop Developing Your Skills

As much as podcasting has changed in recent years, it will develop even more in the years to come. In order to build your career, you will need to continually build your familiarity with new Internet trends and technology, cultural issues, and technical podcasting skills.

You have the tools and connections to get started. Start dreaming and planning. There's no time like the present to start building a career through podcasting!

best practices Actions that professionals agree make a project most effective.

body of work All of the output, in this case podcasts, of a person or group of people in the space of a career.

brainstorm Thinking of all the possibilities for a certain course of action, without stopping to judge whether or not the ideas are good.

consultant Someone who shares his or her expertise on a process or project, often for a fee.

content Words, pictures, or video created for consumption or use by a viewer or reader.

culture The objects, beliefs, and social forms common to a specific population.

idiom A word or phrase that has a special meaning to people in the know.

idiomatic Having a special meaning to people within a specific culture. For example, "TTYL" means "talk to you later" to Internet users and text messagers.

informational interview A meeting between someone working in a profession and someone who would like to work in that same profession. The goal of this interview is to learn more about a company or a position.

marketing The process of advertising and selling a product to distributors, wholesalers, retailers, and consumers.

media Information content delivered via print, audio, video, or other formats.

ping To notify a server that your podcast has been updated.

podcast A Web-based way to broadcast an audio or video recording so that anyone with an MP3 player or personal computer and an Internet connection can receive and play it.

RSS (Really Simple Syndication) The technology that allows listeners to subscribe to and automatically receive a podcast.

tutorial A short class that walks a student through a process or idea. Often used to describe orientations that teach users how to use a specific software program. These are often conducted online.

user-generated content Any words, images, sound files, or video files posted and downloaded by Internet users.

venue A place (real or virtual) that houses your work and makes it available to your audience. For example, Audiophile is a typical venue for podcasters.

viral marketing Getting word out about a product or person by way of Web content that is passed on from user to user. This is often described as "going viral."

voice-over Providing an audio track of your voice reading dialogue for radio or television commercials, narration in films or television shows, animated characters, or re-recorded dialogue.

Web 2.0 The second generation of Internet-based services that include and thrive on user-generated content. This includes social networking sites (such as MySpace), blogs, podcasts, and message boards. In a larger sense, it is the Internet culture that developed when users started sharing their own words, pictures, thoughts, and work with each other online.

white paper An informative article or booklet meant to educate people.

FOR FURTHER READING

Academy of Interactive Arts and Sciences
23622 Calabasas Road, Suite 220
Calabasas, CA 91302
(818) 876-0826
Web site: http://www.interactive.org

Center for Digital Imaging Arts at Boston University
282 Moody Street
Waltham, MA 02453
(781) 209-1700
Web site: http://www.cdiabu.com

Entertainment Software Association
575 7th Street NW, Suite 300
Washington, DC 20004
Web site: http://www.theesa.com

Web Sites

Due to the changing nature of Internet links, Rosen
Publishing has developed an online list of Web sites
related to the subject of this book. This site is updated
regularly. Please use this link to access the list:

http://www.rosenlinks.com/dcb/cbpc

FOR FURTHER READING

Cochrane, Todd. *Podcasting: Do It Yourself Guide.*
Hoboken, NJ: John Wiley & Sons, 2005.

Columbo, George. *Absolute Beginner's Guide to Podcasting.*
Indianapolis, IN: Que Publishing, 2005.

Geoghegan, Michael, and Dan Klass. *Podcast Solutions:
The Complete Guide to Podcasting.* Berkeley, CA:
FriendsofED, 2005.

Jenkins, Henry. "Confronting the Challenges of
Participatory Culture: Media Education for the 21st
Century." The John D. and Catherine T. MacArthur
Foundation. 2006. Retrieved January 24, 2007
(http://www.macfound.org/site/c.lkLXJ8MQKrH/
b.1038727/apps/s/content.asp?ct = 2946895).

Morris, Tee. *Podcasting for Dummies.* New York, NY: For
Dummies, 2005.

BIBLIOGRAPHY

Columbo, George. *Absolute Beginner's Guide to Podcasting.*
Indianapolis, IN: Que Publishing, 2005.

Farkas, Bart G. *Secrets of Podcasting: Audio Blogging
for the Masses.* 2nd ed. Berkeley, CA: Peachpit
Press, 2006.

Gibson, Owen. "Generation Blogger." *Guardian* (UK).
October 16, 2006.

Lee, Felicia R. "Survey of the Blogosphere Finds 12
Million Voices." *New York Times.* July 20,
2006, p. E-3.

Maney, Kevin. "Blend of Old and New Media Launched
OK Go." *USA Today.* November 27, 2006. Retrieved
December 2006 (http://www.usatoday.com/tech/
news/2006-11-27-ok-go_x.htm).

Maney, Kevin. "OK Go: Masters of the YouTube Age."
USA Today. August 29, 2006. Retrieved December
2006 (http://blogs.usatoday.com/maney/2006/
08/ok_go_masters_o.html).

Morris, Tee. *Podcasting for Dummies.* New York, NY: For
Dummies, 2005.

National Center for Missing and Exploited Children.
"Internet Safety Guidelines." MissingKids.com.
Retrieved December 2006 (http://www.missingkids.
com/missingkids/servlet/PageServlet?
LanguageCountry = en_US&PageId = 3026).

Richardson, Will. "Making Waves." *School Library Journal.*
October 1, 2006.

Rumford, Robert L. "Podcasting White Paper: What You Don't Know About Podcasting Could Hurt Your Business: How to Leverage and Benefit from This New Media Technology." Solana Beach, CA: The Info Guru LLC, 2005.

INDEX

P

ping, 39
PodBlaze.com, 37
podcast, name origin, 7
podcasting
  best practices and, 36–45
  as a career, 4, 5, 8, 24–28,
    30–31, 33, 35, 42
  cultural context of, 8–11,
    24, 30
  definition of, 5–6
  distribution, 5, 12, 16, 28, 39
  ease of, 4, 14–16
  free speech and, 6–7, 12
  as a hobby, 4, 24–25
  how-to guide for, 15–20,
    22–23
  keeping records, 16, 50,
    52–53
  musicians and, 4, 15, 47, 49, 50
  other names for, 5
  superstars of, 25–27
  Web 2.0and, 11–12, 24, 39, 46
professionalism, meaning of,
  44–45

Q

Queen Elizabeth II, as a
  podcaster, 4–5

R

RSS (Really Simple
  Syndication), 5, 12,
  16, 39

S

self-publishing, 5–7,
  12, 14
Shoen, Ben, 25
Sims, Andrew, 25

T

tutorials, 38

V

viral marketing, 46–47,
  49–50
voice-over, 30
Voltz, Stephen, 26

W

webcasts, 5, 8
white papers, 37
work ethic, 44

Y

YouTube.com, 49

Z

zines, 6, 12, 14

About the Author

Sarah Sawyer is a content strategist for an electronic media firm in Minneapolis, Minnesota. After ten years working as a professional writer, she is excited to be learning about all of the amazing career opportunities that the Internet provides writers. Her favorite podcasts include Grammar Girl's Quick and Dirty Tips for Better Writing and National Public Radio's This American Life.

Photo Credits

Cover (ipod, laptop, and microphone), p. 1 © www.istockphoto.com; p. 4 © Pool/Anwar Hussein Collection/Getty Images; pp. 6, 17 © Spencer Platt/Getty Images; p. 9 www.istockphoto.com/Mark Stay; p. 10 www.istockphoto.com/Izabela Habur; p. 13 www.istockphoto.com/Lisa Kyle Young; p. 15 © Adam LeJeune; p. 22 © Andrew Cutraro/Getty Images; p. 24 © Gerald S. Williams/Philadelphia Inquirer/MCT/NewsCom.com; p. 29 © Jim Sulley/Newscast/The Image Works; p. 32 © C.C. Chapman/www.cc-chapman.com; p. 41 © Justin Sullivan/Getty Images; p. 45 www.istockphoto.com/marmion; p. 48 © Scott Wintrow/Getty Images; p. 51 (inset) © Soyeon Jung; p. 53 www.istockphoto.com/Zlatko Kostic.

Designer: Nelson Sá
Photo Researcher: Amy Feinberg